D1261520

Learn to DRAW

Drawing
Baby Animals

Jorge Santillan and Sarah Eason

Gareth Stevens
Publishing

Please visit our website, www.garethstevens.com. For a free color catalog of all our high-quality books, call toll free 1-800-542-2595 or fax 1-877-542-2596.

Library of Congress Cataloging-in-Publication Data

Eason, Sarah.
 Drawing baby animals / Sarah Eason.
      pages cm. — (Learn to draw)
ISBN 978-1-4339-9525-5 (pbk.)
ISBN 978-1-4339-9526-2 (6-pack)
ISBN 978-1-4339-9524-8 (library binding)
1. Animals in art—Juvenile literature. 2. Drawing—Technique—Juvenile literature. 3.
Animals—Infancy—Juvenile literature. I. Title.
 NC780.E27 2013
 743.6—dc23
                                        2012048248

Published in 2014 by
Gareth Stevens Publishing
111 East 14th Street, Suite 349
New York, NY 10003

© 2014 Gareth Stevens Publishing

Produced for Gareth Stevens by Calcium Creative Ltd
Illustrated by Jorge Santillan
Designed by Paul Myerscough
Edited by Rachel Blount

Printed in the United States of America

CPSIA compliance information: Batch CS13GS: For further information contact Gareth Stevens, New York, New York at 1-800-542-2595.

Contents

Learn to Draw!

Baby animals are adorable! If you love animal babies, now you can learn how to draw them, too! From kittens and chicks to bunnies, puppies, lambs, and frisky foals, discover the cutest, most lovable babies of the animal world!

You will need:

Just a few simple pieces of equipment are needed to create gorgeous drawings of baby animals:

Sketchpad or paper
Visit an art store to buy good quality paper.

Pencils
You will need both fine-tipped and thick-tipped pencils.

Eraser
Don't worry if you make a mistake—use an eraser to remove any unwanted lines. You can even use it to add highlights.

Paintbrush, paints, and pens
Buy a set of quality paints, brushes, and coloring pens to add color to your adorable drawings.

Playful Puppies

Dogs are loving and fun, and their babies are super sweet! Puppies love to have fun and will play with their owners for hours. Try a game of chase or fetch with a puppy, and it will be your friend forever!

Step 1

Draw your puppy in a crouching pose. Draw the shape of its body, then draw its legs, paws, and tail. Next, draw the puppy's head and ears.

Step 2

Go over the rough lines from step 1 to draw the puppy's outline. Mark the eyes and the nose. Erase the rough lines from step 1.

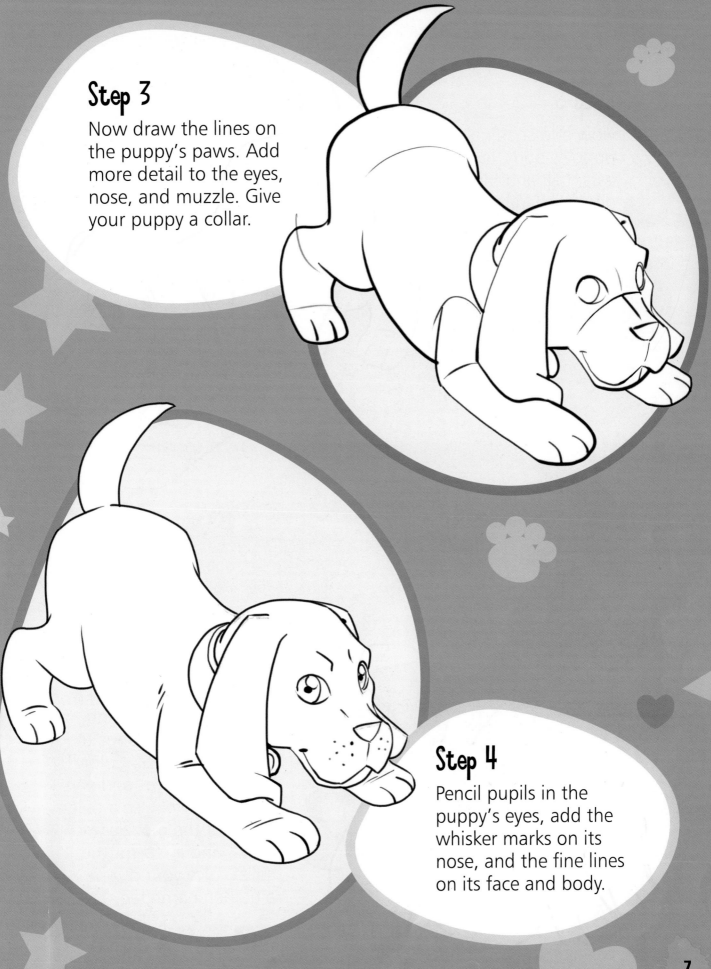

Step 3

Now draw the lines on the puppy's paws. Add more detail to the eyes, nose, and muzzle. Give your puppy a collar.

Step 4

Pencil pupils in the puppy's eyes, add the whisker marks on its nose, and the fine lines on its face and body.

Step 5

Now add shading to your puppy's body, legs, paws, ears, tail, and face. Use deeper shading for the eyes and the nose.

Step 6

Color your puppy with a rich brown shade. Add dark brown markings to the tail and back. Color the puppy's eyes and ears a dark brown. Use a beige color for the muzzle and paws, and a red for the collar. Give your puppy a golden name tag.

Step 7

Now you can put the finishing touches on your puppy. Color its nose dark brown, then add white highlights to the puppy's eyes and brows. Add some highlights to its paws, ears, back, and tail, too. Your cute puppy is complete!

Sleepy Puppies

Like all babies, puppies spend a lot of time sleeping. Baby dogs are born with their eyes shut, and they don't open them until they are around 11 days old! Between 2 and 4 weeks old, puppies start to wag their tails, growl, and bark.

Cute Kittens

Tiny, fluffy, and full of mischief, kittens are great fun to watch. These baby animals are furry balls of energy that love to run around chasing after just about anything!

Step 1

Draw a square for the kitten's head, then draw its legs and body. Use triangles for the kitten's ears, and draw a long, curving "S" shape for its tail.

Step 2

Go over the lines you drew in step 1 to draw the curving outline of the kitten. Erase any unwanted lines, then roughly mark the eyes, paws, and nose.

Step 3

Now add more detail to the face. Draw the shape of the eyes, nose, and mouth. Add the lines on the paws. Draw some fur around the face.

Step 4

Shade the pupils of the eyes. Draw the whiskers and add detail to the shape of the nose. Then draw an oval shape for the kitten's chest.

Step 5

Now add shading to the kitten's head, face, body, legs, and tail. Shade more deeply around the neck and the kitten's belly.

Step 6

Your kitten is a ginger cat! Color it with a rich orange shade, then add the darker orange markings on the head, legs, back, and tail. Color the ears dark orange and the chest, nose, and mouth cream. Color the kitten's eyes green.

Step 7

Add more shading to your kitten's body. Then put highlights on its eyes, chest, paws, tail, and ears to finish your cute and furry friend.

Playful Kittens

Kittens spend lots of time play-fighting each other. It might look like they are just having fun, but this type of play helps baby cats learn how to hunt. Kittens love to play chase games, too. Try wiggling a piece of string across the floor and watch how a kitten darts after it!

Baby Bunnies

With their huge, round eyes, long, soft ears, and twitching noses, it's easy to love baby bunnies! These babies love to be petted and stroked as long as they are handled very gently.

Step 1

Use a rounded shape for your bunny's head. Add two triangular shapes for the ears. Next, draw the body and legs. Then draw the bunny's tail.

Step 2

Go over the lines from step 1 to draw the outline. Erase any unwanted lines. Mark the eye and nose. Add the lines on the head, body, and ears.

Step 3

Now draw the shape of the bunny's eye, nose, and mouth, then add the lines on the paws. Draw the tips of the bunny's ears.

Step 4

Shade the outline and pupil of the eye. Add whiskers and fur lines.

Step 5

Now add shading to your bunny's face, eye, ears, body, and legs. Use darker shading for the eye.

Step 6

Color some of your bunny dark gray, as shown. Use a light pinky-gray for the paler parts of the bunny. Color the bunny's eye a rich, deep red.

Step 7

Now add highlights to your bunny's eye, ears, back, and paws. Color the inside of the ears pink. Add some touches of dark gray for extra shade.

Big Bunny Family

Bunnies have lots of babies. Rabbit moms can have many babies at once, and sometimes up to seven or eight babies at the same time! The group of baby bunnies is called a litter.

Lovable Lambs

Lambs are gentle babies that need lots of loving care from their moms. These babies must drink lots of milk from their mothers after they are born, to help them grow big and strong. Lambs often twitch their fluffy tails as they drink their mom's milk!

Step 1

Draw a rectangular shape for the body. Then draw the legs, neck, and head. Use triangular shapes for the ears and add the tail.

Step 2

Go over the lines you drew in step 1 to give your lamb a rounded outline. Mark the eyes and the nose. Erase any unwanted lines from step 1.

Step 3

Now add the shape of the eyes, nose, and mouth. Add detail to the ears and the hooves.

Step 4

Shade the eyes and add some markings to show the wool on the lamb's legs, body, and tail.

Step 5

Add shading to your lamb's face, ears, legs, and body. Use darker shading for the neck and the inner rear leg.

Step 6

Color your lamb's body, legs, tail, and ears with a beige shade. Leave the head white. Color the hooves dark brown.

Step 7

Color the inside of the ears pink. Then use a deep brown shade for the nose and the mouth. Add a little more shading and some highlights.

Springtime Babies

A female sheep is called a ewe. A ewe will often have more than one lamb at the same time. Some have two babies, called twins. Some even have three lambs, called triplets. Lambs are born in the spring.

Frisky Foals

A baby horse is called a foal. These beautiful baby animals have very long legs—a foal's legs are almost as long as those of a fully grown horse! Foals love to run and jump on their strong, slender legs.

Step 1

Draw a rectangular shape for the foal's body. Then draw its neck, head, legs, and long, curving tail.

Step 2

Pencil a curved outline for your foal. Then erase the rough lines from step 1. Roughly draw the foal's eye, nose, and ears.

Step 3

Add detail to the shape of the legs, hooves, ears, and tail. Draw the shape of the eye and the foal's nostril. Draw the mane, too.

Step 4

Add detail to the foal's mane and add lines to its tail and face. Add the lines on the body.

Step 5

Add depth to your picture by shading the foal's body and face. Use some deeper shading for the inside rear leg, and the foal's eye and neck.

Step 6

Color your foal with a light brown shade. Use a chestnut brown for the mane, tail, and eyes. Color the hooves with a dark brown shade.

Step 7

Now add highlights to the foal's eye, ears, head, body, legs, hooves, and tail. Add some more shading. Your frisky foal is complete!

Growing Up

A male foal is called a colt and a female foal is called a filly. When a foal is 1 year old, it is called a yearling. Baby horses do not become fully grown until they are around 4 or 5 years old.

Cheeping Chicks

Like all baby birds, chicks hatch from eggs laid by their mothers. The mother bird lays her eggs in a nest to keep them safe. The babies break out of their eggs by pecking at them with their beaks.

Step 1

Use circular shapes for the chick's head, body, and the top of its legs. Next, draw the legs and feet. Then draw a triangle for the chick's beak.

Step 2

Go over the rough lines from step 1 to give your chick a rounded outline. Mark the eye and pencil the shape of the feet and wings.

Step 3

Now draw the beak and the shape of the eye. Add feather marks to the wings and add more detail to the chick's feet and claws.

Step 4

Shade the chick's eye and then add detail to its feathers, beak, legs, and feet.

Step 5

Shade your chick's head and body. Add some shading to the legs and feet, too.

Step 6

Use a bright yellow color for the chick's head, wings, and body. Color the legs, feet, and beak orange.

Step 7

Add a touch of blue to your chick's eye, then put some highlights on the head, body, wings, legs, and feet. Add a little more shading, and your cute, cheeping chick is complete!

Fluffy Feathers

Chicks are covered in lots of soft, fluffy feathers called down. The soft feathers keep the tiny baby bird warm. As the chick grows older, it loses its down and instead grows smoother feathers like its mom's.

Glossary

adorable cute and very easy to love

bark the sound a dog or puppy makes to show that it is excited or angry

beak the hard part on a bird's face. Birds use their beaks to peck at things.

dart to move around very quickly

detail the fine lines on a drawing

eggs hard, round objects that are laid by female birds. Baby birds grow within eggs until they are ready to hatch.

erase to remove

fetch to collect something, such as a ball or toy

growl a deep sound that dogs or puppies make when they are scared or angry

hatch to break out of an egg

highlights the light parts on a picture

hooves the hard parts on an animal's feet

hunt to track down an animal for food

laid pushed an egg out of the body

loving full of love and affection

mischief naughty or playful

nest an animal home made of twigs, moss, and other natural objects. Birds make nests in which to lay their eggs.

nostril an opening on an animal's head through which it breathes

pecking tapping at something with a beak. Birds peck with their beaks.

petted stroked and cuddled

pose the position a person or creature is in

shading the dark markings on a picture

slender slim, not fat

spring the season that follows winter. Many baby animals are born in the spring.

twitching moving part of the body very quickly

wag when an animal moves its tail from side to side to show it is happy

For More Information

Books

Ames, Lee J. *Draw 50 Baby Animals: The Step-by-Step Way to Draw Kittens, Lambs, Chicks, Puppies, and Other Adorable Offspring*. New York, NY: Watson-Guptill, 2012.

Ildos, Angela Serena. *Baby Animals: Cube Book*. New York, NY: White Star Publishers, 2010.

Levin, Freddie. *1-2-3 Draw Baby Animals*. London, Canada: Peel, 2006.

Websites

Find out about all kinds of animals on National Geographic's website:
kids.nationalgeographic.com/kids/animals

Discover more about baby animals at:
animal.discovery.com/guides/baby-animals/ baby-animals.html

Learn the names of baby animals at:
www.enchantedlearning.com/subjects/animals/ Animalbabies.shtml

Index